MADDOG:
BUILT FOR WAR

From Block Soldier to Cage Champion

PART 1

BY MARCUS "MADDOG" MORGAN

CONTENTS

PROLOGUE

This ain't no fairytale.
This ain't no sugar-coated, perfect path story.
This is the truth.
My truth.

A life that started dark. Where block life, prison cells, violence and robberies were the norm.

Where loyalty meant everything, and snitches were worse than enemies.

But it's also about change.

Fighting, surviving, chasing.
Losing, suffering, rebuilding.

It's the story of going from a street savage to a champion. Not just in the eyes of the block... but in cages and arenas.

People doubted me, wrote me off and even waited for my downfall.

But I'm still standing. And this story? It's only just beginning.

Read this carefully. You're about to step into my life, completely unfiltered and unglamourised.

This is my journey.

CHAPTER ONE

BORN IN CHAOS

Smethwick. A name heavy with meaning, but never for good reasons.

Where I came from, violence was never shocking. It was expected. Robberies, fights, madness, these were all part of everyday life. Each morning, you awake with a clear choice to either dominate or be dominated. There was no middle ground.

I stamped my presence early. Fighting wasn't optional; it was survival. Disrespect was handled quickly, and arguments often turned physical. People quickly understood that I solved problems with my hands, and my name started building from early on.

But I wasn't reckless for no reason. I moved like a young boss. Always on the block, moving sharp and balancing savagery with being smooth with girls. I could flip the switch fast when needed, and it was that balance that made me stand out.

However, the real birth of 'Maddog' came on a completely different level.

One day, a man let his Pit Bull off the lead on the block. Everyone started to run, except me. I stood solid and stared that dog dead in the eyes. No flinching. No backing off. The dog respected it and backed down, and from that moment, 'Maddog' was born.

I had my own Pit Bull, too. Trixie. She was incredibly loyal and protective, just like me, and anywhere I went, you would see her close by.

By the time I was nineteen, I was no longer pretending. I was Maddog - not just by name, but by definition, too.

I was respected, feared, and most of all, ready for whatever might come my way.

Arguments no longer ended in words, confrontation was never avoided and on the block, when tension rose, people looked to me first. I wasn't chasing clout. I didn't need to. My reputation was built naturally from scars, from silence, and from the way I carried myself.

No backing down. No snitching. No weakness.

But I wasn't wild for no reason. There was always structure to it, and even in complete madness, I still made sure I moved smartly. I hustled because I had to, and it was never about designer clothes or expensive chains but about making sure those nearest to me were able to eat. My family, my friends and the block were all I cared about.

However, deep down, I knew the small street money was never going to be enough, and I was always hungry for more. I wanted to move bigger, smarter, and colder.

I was already Maddog, but soon, Maddog needed to become something even greater, and that's when the next chapter started writing itself.

Not through talk, though. Through action.

CHAPTER TWO

CLOSING TIME GANG

I came home in 2013 having served prison time for a stabbing. Everything on the block was the same as I had left it, but there was a change in me. I could see the same faces, the same slow money and the same small moves and quickly realised it was no longer me. My mind had shifted, and I wanted more.

"Shotting's done. We need serious money," I told the mandem – and when Maddog spoke, things moved fast.

By 2014, it was no longer an idea or talk on the block. It was action. We had built a tight squad — four solid members and a trusted driver. Our targets were serious; post offices, banks and supermarkets (mostly Asda) were frequently hit. We weren't aiming for the tills or petty loose change. We were after the safes - big bags or nothing. There was no in-between.

We became known as the Closing Time Gang as we always hit them just before closing hours when the staff were tired, and security was at its lightest. The hits were ruthless but always controlled. We would pull up clean, masks on and gloves tight. A cool, calm, but firm presence.

"Everyone down. No games." that was always the first line.

We played our roles well. One would lock the doors so no one could enter or leave, two would manage the staff and make sure no one wanted to be a hero, while one would enter the safe and take everything they could.

Anyone who tried to delay things or get in the way was roughed up. I remember one time a manager stalled and didn't do as we demanded, so he (along with the rest of his staff) was dragged into the freezer and locked in there while we got to work clearing the safe.

Cold? Definitely. But to me, this was business. The safes in Asda were always the easiest wins as we could quickly get the key, open the door and BOOM. Thousands of pounds just sitting there at our mercy.

After every hit, the adrenaline was always pumping heavily. We would jump back in the car, laughing, hyped up and buzzing with the score. Each time it felt like another easy win, and we would think, "shit, we could do this all day!" But big moves bring the heat.

While the rest of the block saw us as kings and the youngers rated us, some of the olders were watching on with jealousy; however, no one stepped on our toes or tried to stop us. Police pressure was starting to get heavy, though. ANPR hits. Close chases. One night, things nearly became fatal, and we were minutes from losing our freedom and maybe even our lives. That night stayed with me.

There were sirens everywhere. My heart was beating faster than it had ever done before. the driver was shaking with adrenaline but remained focused. Our masks were half off, and the money bags were stacked behind us. So far, so normal. Then, looking out the window, the entire street was suddenly illuminated as the blues and twos were lit up.

Fuck. One wrong turn now, and we were finished. But we moved smart. Ditched the car behind an estate, switched clothes in record time, dumped our gloves and phones and were away on our toes. By the time the armed response reached the area, we were ghosts, sitting in our local trap spot, acting like regular people looking out the window with money on our minds.

That was the game. Cold. Ruthless. Surgical. But even ghosts leave shadows.

The streets started to talk, and police pressure tightened. Every day, undercover cars would roll past, our phones were being tapped, and road cameras were monitored extensively, clocking our faces, cars and movements.

Still, inside our circle? We felt untouchable. The block loved us; money was building up and every robbery was feeling smoother and more in control. We were getting cocky.

But that's the thing about the streets. You don't always get caught when you're sloppy, you're far more likely to be caught when you feel unstoppable. Yet despite everything, deep down, I still didn't fear the police, but it was the fear of betrayal that stayed with me.

The snakes weren't just outside. They were next to us.

I didn't know it yet, but loyalty was about to get tested in ways none of us expected. And I was about to learn that when snakes show teeth, they bite. Hard.

CHAPTER THREE

BETRAYAL
AND THE FALL

Success attracts snakes. Not outsiders. Insiders.

One bredrin, someone I trusted fully and ate with, rode with and even rapped with, would prove to be one such snake and would turn to the dark side, poisoned by jealousy.

After the police grabbed him, he folded fast. Despite not facing any heavy pressure, he caved and sang like a canary. In the cold interview room, he broke down. With a shaky voice and darting eyes, he told the police everything they wanted to hear.

"Yeah… Maddog and them…" Names. Cars. Patterns. Given up instantly.

While he folded, we stayed solid, but the raid would hit just a few days later. Not because the police were smart and had finally caught up with us but because betrayal had opened the door.

This hurt deeply. You expect rats from enemies, not people you classed as family. But I stayed patterned and ghosted while he folded.

However, ghosts can't hide forever, and police pressure became heavy. Raids. Door crashes. Undercover cars. There were eyes everywhere, and one by one, each one of us was grabbed. Some were caught slipping, some were surprised at home. Me? I stayed moving smart and for six months, I became a shadow. Changing cars, switching spots, keeping low, I was impossible to find.

But even shadows get caught in the light.

One close call nearly ended it early. They raided my girl's yard while I was right there. Thankfully, I remained calm and sat there as they walked in. They looked me dead in the face and asked. "Who are you?" I stayed silent. I knew them, this was rushed intel.

No panic. No slip. No picture. No proof.

They searched, pressed me for details and waited, but they had nothing. While the minutes felt like hours, they eventually let me go and I walked out calmly. Freedom still mine.

The thing about betrayal, though, is that it doesn't stop once it starts sliding, and I soon found myself hit again. The snake had talked too much and by now, they knew everything they needed, and it all came crashing down around me. I got caught.

The case was loaded and I quickly found myself in court, stood in that dock solid as the judge read out I would be spending the next seven years inside. The judge dropped it on me like it was light.

My family cried. My girl broke. My circle shattered. Me? I remained stone cold. Unlike those I thought were friends, I didn't snitch, beg or fold. I went down how I wanted, with my head held high and knowing deep down that this wasn't the end of Maddog. This was just another war, and I was ready to fight it.

CHAPTER FOUR

JAIL: WHERE WARRIORS ARE MADE

Prison doesn't care who you are on the roads. Maddog? That name was just noise unless I backed it up in blood. Early on, jail was chaos in HD. You could forget about comfort; this was war every day.

Arguments would turn violent in seconds. Screws kicking off doors. Shouts through vents all night. Blood on the floors regularly. It was tough. Segregation became a familiar sight, and isolation wasn't punishment — it was normal.

I didn't land and chill. I was shipped around like a parcel, I went to seven different jails. Seven different battle zones. Each one with its own rules, politics and predators. Some days, you settle; others you would arrive straight in the middle of war.

I remember landing at one spot, and I didn't even have time to unpack before a man tried to test me. They swung first, but it didn't matter. Fists flew, bones cracked, and blood sprayed on plastic chairs. I patterned them quickly, fast and violent. That was the language here.

Dominoes slammed 24/7. Phones buzzed in the shadows. Weed smoked through twisted sheets. Arguments lit wings up like wildfire. It was dog eat dog. I kept my burner phone close, which allowed me to speak to my block, my girl (who remained loyal), and my mum, who stayed strong (although I could hear her voice crack sometimes).

Jail broke many, I saw it regularly. Self-harm became normal, blades would slice across arms, blood dripping down sinks, screws dragging bodies out limp. Suicides too. No fantasy.

People really lost themselves in here.

But me? That wasn't my story. Maddog stayed sharp and savage but boredom crept in. The same routines, tension and madness got tedious. There's no medals for surviving jail, so I flipped it and made my own war.

Fight Club. My idea, my rules. This wasn't for money or power, though. It was for me. Fighting was easy, it's what I had always known and was what kept me alive. The screws didn't know, they couldn't. This was run by inmates, with no gloves or mats, just violence.

You had beef or pride? Step in and get it sorted. Fists would fly, noses would break, and eyes would swell while the walls were splashed in blood. People respected it, though. No rats, no weapons, just realness.

I didn't lose. Not even once.

But even through the punches and knockouts… something deeper crawled into my head at night. Silence. Darkness. Left alone with my thoughts I would often think, "Is this it? Is this really life forever?" I'd stare at cracked ceilings, listening to rats scratching and running on the landing while men cried in the dark begging on their phones and suicide watches were called at 3 am. Jail didn't scare me, but wasting my life did.

Marcus the Fighter wasn't born yet, but something had started loading. It wasn't loud or screaming, it was patient. Waiting.

Maddog survived jail, there was never any doubt in that, but when the gates opened? Marcus was ready to take his first steps… and that was when the next war would begin.

CHAPTER FIVE

THE SWITCH

Just because I had my freedom, it didn't mean I had peace. It was 2018, I had a fresh home, and I thought this time would be different. I told myself the streets wouldn't pull me back, but the block has a way of calling your name. It's loud when you're back, soft when you're gone, but it's always there.

The block stayed active. The beef stayed alive. The ops stayed hungry.

Weeks earlier, me and the mandem had mashed up some boys, it was just regular block business and how disrespect was answered. That's just how we moved. However, the streets don't hand out warnings, and that night changed everything.

I was walking home alone. It was late and cold, and the streets were empty. The silence was loud. Too loud. That's when I clocked it: a car. Creeping along, no plates and no lights. It was ops. It's in these moments when your body feels before your brain can think. I kept walking, keeping my eyes sharp and my breathing slow. Then? Gunfire.

Three sharp cracks tore through the silence.

BANG.

BANG.

BANG.

Bullets zipped past my head, close. Too close. I didn't drop, though. I didn't scream or run. I froze. Not out of fear — out of calculation, "Shit… this is real". I could feel the air shift as those shots missed me by inches, and one mistake, I wouldn't be here telling this story.

They sped off fast, their tyres screaming into the distance as they left me standing there, my heart thumping and mind racing.

The silence returned, but this time it felt different. It was heavy and dark. "That could've been it," I whispered to myself and in that moment, I should've felt lucky, but I didn't. I felt rage, and I wanted revenge.

Maddog was still alive. He was still breathing heavily inside me and was ready to load up and ride out. Life had other plans, though. Probation clocked the shooting fast, but they didn't care about details or even that I was the target. All they needed was my name and that was enough to see me cuffed up and back in side, no arguments.

There I was in another cold cell doing another stretch. But this one? This one hit differently. Not because I was scared or because I was broken but because I was tired. I was tired of the cycle, of the waster years, of sitting in a cell while life outside kept moving without me.

I remember sitting on that concrete bed, my hands folded and eyes staring at walls I'd seen too many times before. For the first time, I admitted it to myself, "Jail? I'm done with it."

The roads were still in me, still burning deep, but something else was whispering now. MMA. Not the belts, fame or glory, but the idea. If I was going to fight, I needed to do it properly. There would be no more scrapping for ego or beefing with people for no reason. Fighting would need to mean something.

The switch flipped right there in that tiny, freezing cell. Maddog was still alive, he always would be, but when I walked out the next time, I was not going to waste it. I was going to make war my profession.

CHAPTER SIX

FIGHTING FOR A NEW LIFE

After being recalled for the shooting and spending another twenty months inside, something inside me had changed. I wasn't scared, and I wasn't broken. But I was tired. Tired of wasting years, of giving my life to the system, watching everything move forward while I was stuck behind bars.

Jail was finished for me. The roads? They still had a grip. Still calling my name. But something was shifting deep inside. Fighting had always been there, from block wars to prison punch-ups, but what if I flipped that energy and used it for something bigger?

That's when MMA loaded in my mind. Not for belts or fame. Not yet. Just for direction, purpose, and critically, escape.

When I came home after that twenty-month stretch, I stayed focused. I didn't slip — not even a week, I stayed clean for nine solid months. I kept ghost, avoiding the madness, but unfortunately the world had other plans.

COVID hit. Gyms shut down, fights were cancelled, and opportunities vanished overnight. It frustrated me. I was finally ready to leave the road behind, but the world had pressed pause. The block didn't care about COVID though. Money still moved, and friends still called.

"Bro, easy moves about. Pattern this."

Temptation continued to circle heavily, but deep down, I knew the truth. If I was to go back now, I would be finished. So I stayed locked in, focusing on home workouts and studying fights all while running solo. That became my new normal.

Still, old street trouble would catch up with me again. Another case landed on my name. I wasn't directly involved, but when my name was linked, I stood tall. No snitching. No talking. I held the weight and got sentenced again — twenty final months.

That last stretch felt different. Jail didn't scare me anymore. It bored me. Every night I sat in my cell repeating the same thing to myself. "When I'm out, I'm gone from all this. MMA or nothing."

When they finally opened that door, I didn't waste a second. I went straight from the gates to the MMA gym. No chilling. No delays. But stepping into that gym hit different. This wasn't the block or a jail cell. This was discipline.

The air smelled of sweat and hard work. The mats were clean and lined perfectly. Coaches stood sharp, watching everything, while everyone in there looked like killers in their own right. They were focused and ready.

I paused for a moment. For the first time in years, I felt anxiety slap me hard. This wasn't street fear, but something else entirely. "Do I belong here?" I thought to myself. That voice crept into my mind - I wasn't wearing chains, rolling with mandem backed by noise or clout. This was me, alone. Marcus, not Maddog. Suddenly, all the past violence felt small. This wasn't about being loud or wild, it was about skill, respect and sacrifice. I stood frozen for a second. Breathing shallow. Mind racing.

Could I really do this?

But Maddog doesn't fold. Never has. That side of me kicked in quickly. "Fuck that," I said, "Let's work" - and from that moment, I didn't stop. I trained harder than everyone. Pain became normal. Sore muscles, bruised ribs, sweat puddles on the mats — I embraced it all.

Ghost Mode switched on. No parties. No block calls. No distractions. Just discipline and war.

It paid off fast. In 2022, my MMA debut was set, I would be fighting Jordan Wheater. Fight night came fast, and the block rolled deep, over a hundred strong. Loud and proud, the whole building shook when I walked out. The lights were blinding, smoke filling the air, cameras flashing everywhere. I could feel my name bounce through the walls, but as they locked that cage door, the pressure hit me again.

This wasn't jail. This wasn't the block. This was the cage. Here, there were no ops or mandem backing me, it was just me, and I was all alone. As the ref shouted, "FIGHT!", Maddog switched on instantly and I went full savage. There was no feeling-out or patience, I rushed Jordan fast with a mix of combinations, power shots, hooks and uppercuts; he couldn't land a single punch.

Jordan became a victim in seconds. His legs stiff, eyes lost, he realised this wasn't his level. Forty-five seconds later, it was done. The ref jumped in, and I took my maiden first round TKO. I instantly lost it, spinning around to the crowd, screaming at the top of my lungs, "THIS IS MY FUCKING CAGE!"

The block exploded. Phones flashed, mandem roared, and I walked around like a lion that had just killed in front of his pack. Jordan stayed slumped, still processing the storm.

I had arrived.

Maddog wasn't gone; he never will be, but now he lived in a new world. This wasn't about street fights anymore. This was my cage. And I was running it.

CHAPTER SEVEN

BETWEEN TWO WORLDS

The cage was now my stage and after my savage debut, life felt different. People looked at me differently. I wasn't just Maddog from Smethwick anymore, I was Maddog the fighter, the winner. Mandem who hadn't spoken to me in years were back on the line, old friends popping up like they had never been away. Everyone wanted a piece of me now.

The block celebrated like they won the fight themselves. My name rang everywhere. Even people outside the ends started watching. From the estates to the raves, Maddog was now a name that carried weight in two worlds... and I can't lie — it felt good.

Respect wasn't something I had to demand anymore. It walked in before I did. Even without moving wild, my presence still spoke for itself. The streets rated me heavy, and the roads held my name tight, even though I was barely outside anymore.

At the same time, music was booming again. "Robbery Lane" dropped and caught fire fast. The streets related because it was real, and I wasn't faking anything in my lyrics. I rapped what I lived. I told my story raw, and people connected.

Suddenly, I wasn't just Maddog the fighter. I was Maddog the artist, too. MMA in the day and Studio vibes at night. I had people pushing me to take music seriously, and fans would constantly message me while DJs were spinning my tracks and the roads singing along.

But success is a tricky thing. Wherever it goes, temptation follows. As nights out became regular again and promoters hollered, clubs started to give me the VIP treatment. The raves welcomed me heavy, and bottles flowed endlessly while girls moved loose, and old faces tried to remind me of old moves. I got caught up. I wasn't fully back in the streets, but close enough even though I thought I had it patterned.

"I'm still Maddog. I can live both lives." I would say to myself, but deep down, I could feel cracks slowly starting to show. Training felt lighter and sessions were missed here and there. Late nights turning into sluggish mornings and discipline slipped before I could even realise.

Still, the next fight came fast. December 2022. My second MMA bout was booked, and I stayed confident. In my head? Easy work. I was running through this guy like Jordan. I even made my own walkout track again; the fighter and the rapper blending together. I was convinced I was unstoppable.

Fight week came and everything felt patterned. But on the day, something felt different. I wasn't as sharp. Not physically or mentally. The nightlife, the distractions, the ego, it was all starting to weigh me down, but as soon as the lights came on, I switched back into Maddog mode.

The opponent had talked heavy all week, saying how he was going to test me and thought boxing would save him. He had no idea who he was stepping in with. When the cage door shut, the street came out of me again.

The first round was calm and while he moved smart, I stalked and waited. By the second round, the switch flipped. I mauled him. Clinch, pressure, heavy hands, ground and pound, I was relentless. He couldn't breathe. He couldn't think. I made him drown in violence. The ref had no choice but to wave it off. A second-round TKO, another win and another night for the block to scream about.

I jumped up like a king. Another victim handled. The whole arena felt my energy. I left that cage high on confidence, I was 2-0 in MMA with back-to-back finishes. The streets roaring for me. The music moving numbers. Everything running smooth. Or so I thought.

But behind all the celebrations, a quiet truth was creeping in. I wasn't living right, and I wasn't locked in properly. I still had one foot in each world. While the cage gave me discipline, the block gave me ego, and I was walking a thin line and just couldn't see how dangerous it was becoming.

The ends still called me heavy. Friends ringing for moves. Clubs inviting me back in. Everyone wanted Maddog. Not Marcus. I was winning, running the cage, but the cracks were getting bigger in the background and soon, they were going to break wide open.

CHAPTER EIGHT

THE REALITY CHECK

Success can blind you and after my second MMA win, life felt different. I wasn't just Maddog from the block anymore. I was Maddog the fighter. Maddog the winner. Everywhere I went, I could feel the shift. Mandem were back around. Old friends popped up again. People who hadn't spoken to me in years now acted like family. My name was ringing everywhere… and I can't lie, it felt good.

Respect followed me heavily and I didn't have to demand it. It arrived before I even said a word. The streets still held my name strong, even though I wasn't outside as much. At the same time, my music was moving, "Robbery Lane" had dropped and caught fire and the streets felt it because it was real. Every bar came from the life I'd actually lived.

Suddenly, I wasn't just Maddog the fighter. I was Maddog the storyteller too. MMA by day, studio and block love by night. Everything was clicking. I had the cage. I had the roads. I had the music, but success brings temptation.

I found myself outside, and nights out became routine again. I was everywhere — clubs, raves, carnivals. You name it, I was there. If there was a motive, I pulled up, and every weekend felt like a movie. Bottles popped, music blasting, girls moving mad, and block energy all over the room.

I wasn't running clubs. I was living in them. Everywhere I went, love followed. Pictures, salutes, girls showing wild attention - I got caught up. I wasn't soft, nor dumb I was just too comfortable. In my head, I convinced myself it was sweet, "I'm still Maddog. I can live both lives" but quietly, the cracks were starting to show.

Late nights turning into slow mornings. The sharp edge was blunting, and I didn't even realise. Then the big opportunity came. A promoter came forward, he had seen the hype and the numbers I could pull so offered me a title fight. Not just a normal scrap. A real belt, a real crown. My name alone sold tickets, and he knew it.

I didn't hesitate. I jumped on it. In my mind, this was easy maths. Road experience + six months training + hunger = championship. The fight date made it sweeter - February 19th, My birthday. I told myself this was destiny, but life doesn't play by your script.

Fight camp came and went and looking back now it was clear I wasn't locked in properly. Nights out mixed with training meant my recovery wasn't sharp and the hunger wasn't pure. But I didn't care. I believed I'd turn up and get it done like always.

Fight night arrived. It was a new city, a new crowd and I remember standing backstage, gloves tight, head nodding, and music playing, when nerves started to creep in. This wasn't home. This wasn't the block. This was neutral ground.

As I walked out, I tried to carry Maddog energy, but deep inside, doubt was whispering. The cage door shut, all the noise faded, and it was now just me and him. Right away, I knew this wouldn't be easy. He came sharp and didn't respect my name. He wasn't backing down and didn't care about my block wins or my music numbers. He came to fight.

It turned into war fast, five rounds of utter madness. Back and forth, he landed clean shots, and I returned fire. The crowd and commentators were on edge and every round felt 50/50. My body started slowing, my shots weren't landing clean anymore and by round five, we were both feeling it. Bruised up. Faces swollen. Limbs heavy.

Every movement hurt. My shots lost sharpness and in the end it was grit and willpower that carried us through. There were no shortcuts or faking this one, it was real. Finally, the bell rang, and it was done. I looked at him. He looked at me. Both of us knew — it was close.

But deep down? I felt it. I hadn't done enough.

The announcer read the decision. His hand went up – my first loss. I stood there, silent. Not broken or angry, just still. Inside though, it stung deep. This wasn't meant to happen. I left the cage, pretending it was cool, but the cameras didn't catch the real pain. I smiled on the outside but inside, I was raging. I didn't take it well.

What did I do? Same old Maddog. I partied. That night, straight from the cage, I hit the rave. Still sweaty from the fight. Bottles were flowing, girls were everywhere, and loud music drowned out my thoughts. But the doubt had already crept in. I could tell people were whispering. The block can turn quick.

"Is Maddog really him though?"

"Lost now. Too much outside."

I acted like it didn't bother me. But it did. The cracks were no longer hidden. They were showing. That loss wasn't just on the record. It was on my soul. A wake-up call. The cage didn't care about my past or respect my name. It only respected discipline and those who lived the grind every day.

I knew something had to change and that first loss wasn't the end. It was simply the start of the harshest lesson I'd ever learn.

CHAPTER NINE

THE FALL BEFORE THE RISE

Losing once? You get over it. Losing twice? People start whispering. Losing three times in a row? That's when they stop whispering and start laughing.

I had always been known as the guy who couldn't be broken. From the roads to prison to the cage, I had built a reputation of being unshakable. But losing back-to-back-to-back shook me in ways I hadn't felt before. I didn't even need social media or people's mouths to confirm it. I knew the look and could feel the shift in energy. People started moving differently and calls became quieter. Support started fading and the respect that once came easy suddenly felt distant. Even my own thoughts turned dark.

After the third loss, I couldn't even pretend anymore. I left the arena that night silent. No smiles or false confidence. Just a heavy cloud hanging over me. I sat in the car staring out the window, numb. Music played low in the background, but I wasn't hearing it. In that moment, I wasn't Maddog. I was just Marcus. A man who knew he let himself slip too far.

The hardest part wasn't losing. Fighters lose every day. The hardest part was knowing I hadn't given everything I could. That's what burned the most. Not that my opponents were better but that I let them beat me because I was only showing 60% of myself.

Deep down, I knew this was all my fault. I tried pushing the pain down at first and stayed active, still showing face here and there and acting like I wasn't bothered. But inside, I was falling apart quietly. The confidence was gone. The hunger felt drained. I doubted myself and at times questioned everything.

"Maybe I'm done."

"Maybe MMA's not for me."

"Maybe this was all hype and I've been exposed."

These weren't just passing thoughts, they stayed sitting in my head every day, heavy like weights that I just couldn't lift. The block? Silent. Music? I didn't care about writing. Friends? Most disappeared, like they always do when you're not winning.

For the first time in years, I found myself fully alone and that's when the switch flipped. Because in that silence, without crowds or clout or fake supporters, I remembered who I really was. Not the version of Maddog the block knew or the guy living nightlife heavy. The raw version. The prison-hardened, pressure-made fighter that had survived cages long before MMA ever knew my name.

I realised something simple but powerful: no one was going to save me or hand me back the respect. If I wanted to rise again, I had to strip everything down and rebuild from scratch, which meant cutting people off, shutting down all distractions and going ghost for real.

And I did. I disappeared. Not in a petty way — in a surgical way. Phones were ignored, the studio was dark, and there were no clubs, carnivals or loose company. I locked myself into training like my life depended on it. Because in many ways, it did.

I suffered quietly. I sweated alone. No cameras. No applause. The pain of those losses became my fuel. Every round, every rep, every drill, I carried them on my back. Day by day, brick by brick, I rebuilt Maddog into something smarter, sharper, and deadlier. Because this time? I wasn't chasing hype. I wasn't balancing lives. I wasn't half-hearted. This time, I was coming back for war and war doesn't allow comfort.

By the end of that year, after months of pure isolation and grind, I knew I was ready and while the world thought I had fallen off for good, in the shadows I had become something dangerous again.

The comeback was loading — and soon, the cage would witness what silent suffering builds.

CHAPTER TEN

THE COMEBACK BEGINS

Ghost mode. It sounds simple when you say it, but living it is another thing. Ghost mode strips you down and takes away the noise, the love, and the distractions. You find out who you really are in that silence.

After my third straight loss, I vanished from everything. The fight cards, the parties, the block it was all gone. The hype faded quickly, and the calls slowed down. The support disappeared. For years, I had lived loud. Now, my world was quiet. No more clubs. No more carnivals. No outside.

Just me, cold mornings, long runs, aching muscles, and brutal self-reflection.

At first, I hated it. I wasn't used to the quiet. I wasn't used to moving without being seen or rated. But slowly, I realised this was the only way. I couldn't fake this comeback or shortcut my way back to the top. I had to rebuild properly.

Doubt stayed heavy in my head. Every day I battled thoughts of quitting. Of walking away. "Maybe I'm done." "Maybe they were right." But as painful as those thoughts were, they pushed me. They kept me working. And quietly, as months passed, the hunger returned. Not for clout. Not for belts. But for self-respect. I wanted to know, for myself, if I was really built for this.

During this rebuilding stage, I also found balance. A girl from my school days had come back into my life, and for once, things weren't about hype or the streets. She didn't care about Maddog. She cared about Marcus and that grounded me. Gave me a clearer head as I trained harder than ever.

Then, the phone call came: March 2024, Robin Charlton, a tough game fighter who was known for being solid, durable, and aggressive. This was my chance. Not to silence the world, but to silence my own doubts, and I accepted instantly.

Fight night arrived quickly and this time it felt different. There was no wild energy or block mentality. Just focus. No crowd hype or chasing knockouts, I was locked in, and when the cage door shut, it felt cold. Clinical. Exactly how I wanted it.

Robin came out fast. He was aggressive and pressed forward heavily, looking to test me. But this wasn't the old Maddog. I didn't bite on every feint. I didn't swing wild to impress the crowd. I stayed sharp and smart.

My jab landed clean, I controlled the range, used my footwork, and picked my shots carefully. By the end of the first round, I had established control and entering round two, Robin tried to push harder, but I stayed composed. Every time he tried to make it ugly, I calmed it down and made him miss. I punished him with clean counters and kept him frustrated.

Round three was all about closing the show professionally. No risks, no mistakes. I controlled him again, worked the body and legs, and outclassed him to the final bell.

When the fight ended, I knew what it was: a unanimous decision, a complete clean sweep. I was back. But even as the referee raised my hand, I could feel it in the air… "Okay, good win, but is Maddog really back?"

Some fans wanted a knockout. Some doubted if a decision win meant I was fully restored. I knew that. I could hear it without them saying it, but I didn't care. This win wasn't for them or for my highlight reels. This was about proving to myself that when I go ghost, when I sacrifice, and when I lock in, I can beat solid opponents and move forward.

Walking out of that cage, I felt something pure. I was no longer looking around for validation or screaming and playing up to the camera, I just knew, quietly, that I was on the right track again.

This wasn't the redemption yet, though. This was just the initial spark and now it was lit, the fire was only going to grow. Maddog was back on the win column, but the true comeback had only just begun.

CHAPTER ELEVEN

FROM
SPARK TO FLAME

The win against Robin was necessary but it wasn't satisfying. Sure, it shut up the doubts in my head, but not fully in the air. A decision win is solid, but it doesn't scare people, and many people still asked whether I could finish fights.

Deep down, I knew that too. I knew what they meant. I didn't come back just to scrape by, I came back to remind people that I was still dangerous. So after Robin, I stayed sharp. No partying. No distractions. I went back into savage mode. Mornings on the road running. Afternoons on the mats drilling. Nights watching tape until my eyes hurt.

I wasn't chasing cameras anymore. I was chasing the best version of myself and then came the next step. The next test. May 17th, 2024.

The next fight was booked fast and this one felt important. The Robin win proved I belonged in the cage, and this one needed to prove I was still a threat. However, even before fight night, tension sparked. At weigh-ins, my opponent missed weight – and not by a little bit. He came in heavy by a few kilos. That's disrespectful in this game, it's basically saying, "I'm bigger than you, and I'll bully you."

That flicked a switch inside me. I didn't argue or make noise. I stayed silent and smiled. "You'll pay for that tomorrow," I thought to myself, and as fight night arrived I was ready. The crowd wasn't massive, but it didn't need to be. I wasn't here for cheers anymore, I was here for business.

When the cage door shut, I was calm. Cold. Calculated. He came out aggressively, as expected. Bigger, heavier, trying to pressure, but this wasn't emotional Maddog anymore. I didn't swing wild or try to brawl. I didn't throw a single punch. I stayed sharp and let him come forward wildly. Then I shot clean, fast, and smooth, the takedown landed perfectly and now he was in my world.

Within seconds, I had found the opening: his neck. He was there for the taking and I snatched it like lightning. I got him in a guillotine choke, a tight, fast, and vicious move that gave him no space and nowhere to escape. He tried to fight and tried to roll but it didn't matter.

He tapped fast, within 39 seconds, without any punches thrown. Just a cold, calculated death choke that ended it instantly.

I stood up quietly. No wild celebrations. But inside? That felt huge. That wasn't luck, or scraping by. That was domination. A heavier man, a disrespectful weigh-in, it was all Irrelevant. I ended him clinically and fast.

Walking out of the cage, I felt the shift again. This time, no one could doubt it. Two fights back, the first a decision and now a first round finish in 39 seconds. The flame wasn't flickering anymore, it was burning bright and others in the division were about to feel it.

That said, I still wasn't screaming for belts just yet, although I knew they were coming. Maddog wasn't surviving anymore, he was hunting again.

CHAPTER TWELVE

SETBACKS AND STAYING LOCKED

Momentum was finally on my side again. I'd had two fights and two wins, including one brutal, fast finish. Everything felt back on track and now? Belts were loading. This was where I was always supposed to be, and the next opportunity came fast: The title shot.

I accepted it immediately without hesitation. I knew this was the next step and the talk was done. The comeback had been proven and now it was time to crown myself properly.

But nothing in fighting is promised.

As camp was kicking in properly, bad news came crashing in. My opponent had pulled out with an injury to his shoulder, the same old story and the fight was off. I can't lie, I was fuming. All that sacrifice, all that focus, wasted. I stayed calm on the outside, but inside I was boiling. I had been locked in for this moment. But I understood.

This wasn't the roads. This wasn't street life where you show up no matter what. Fighting is different. If you're injured, the fight can't happen. I didn't like it, but I accepted it and with no date in place, I made a decision that I would recharge properly, which is when Jamaica came calling.

In November 2024, I flew out and gave myself something rare, some peace. For two weeks, I switched everything off. No gym. No drills. No early runs. Just pure living. Yacht parties, laughs with friends, mad good food and relaxed days on beaches. It was pure freedom and for a little while, I enjoyed life properly.

But even with vibes flowing, I couldn't lie. The title fight stayed heavy in my mind. At night, when the noise died down, it spoke to me. I wasn't done yet and when December came, I flew home and straight away, reality slapped me… I stepped on the scales and saw 76kg.

Heavy.

The holiday had done its job — but now it was time to do mine. The title fight wasn't dead. It was back on for February 15th, 2025. I was locked in. This wasn't just another fight. This was tension. This was pressure. This was for my first ever amateur belt.

Everything I had done, every risk, every sacrifice, every fall and rebuild had all led here. My chance to win real gold. My chance to crown this comeback properly. I didn't hesitate. Camp started instantly and ghost mode was switched back on. I followed a strict diet, trained hard and put in some painful sessions to burn off that holiday weight. Some days were brutal, and my body felt sluggish early on, but the hunger was serious and every rep, every early morning, every uncomfortable cut felt worth it because this time it wasn't about proving I belonged, it was about becoming champion.

By fight week, I was ready. Tight. Sharp. Focused. Walking out to the cage, the lights hit me differently this time. This wasn't excitement. This wasn't nerves. This was destiny.

I stepped into the cage. Gloves tight, breathing slow, everything was silent now. Then I turned and saw him, my opponent, the last man standing in front of my dream. As the referee closed the cage door, the metal slammed shut. There was no more time for talking or preparing, it was me, him, and everything on the line.

We stared at each other. Eyes locked, serious and cold. This wasn't about hype anymore. This was about everything.

"Fighters ready?"

I nodded. This was it.

CHAPTER THIRTEEN

CROWNED IN BLOOD

The cage door slammed shut and the silence hit differently. I could tell this wasn't just another fight. This wasn't just another opponent. This was it, everything I had worked for since leaving the roads, all that rebuilding after losses, all that grinding through lonely nights.

My first amateur title on the line and I stared across at him, he was fully focused and serious, just like me. The ref gave his final instructions. No smiles. No words. Just eyes locked. The bell rang, round one.

He came out sharp, faster than I expected and got straight into movement, using his kicks smartly. The low kicks hit early as he tried to slow me down. I stayed composed, though, and kept reading his movements, breaking him down piece by piece.

Then he threw a high kick. Fast. Clean. I defended tightly and blocked it perfectly. I the saw an opening and reacted by trying to jump guard and pull him into my world. But he adjusted fast and caught me in a triangle choke, a tight and dangerous move. His legs were locked tight around my neck and the pressure built instantly. I could hear the crowd roar and even the commentators felt the danger.

"Maddog might be in serious trouble here!"

But did I panic? No. I stayed patient and calm under fire and slowly worked my way out. Bit by bit I was able to find a gap and as I popped my head free, the momentum instantly flipped. I stayed on top and made him pay for that risky and heavy move by grounding and pounding with all I had before the bell. Those sharp and clean shots reminded him, the commentators and the audience that I'm still here.

As the bell rang. I stood confidently and could notice he stood slower now. His big moment had come and gone, it was my time. Back in the corner, my coach was direct, "Good escape. Now break him," he said.

As round two rang out, I came out ready to finish. Early into the round, we clashed hard and ended up in the pocket trading blows. He tried his best, swinging wildly in an attempt to knock me out but it was pure desperation. That's when it happened. His shoulder popped.

Mid-exchange, his body had given out and he pulled back awkwardly, clearly hurt. I saw it straight away, but didn't care. This was not the time for sympathy, we're in a war here. He tried to hang on, even attempting to pull guard again. Desperate. But I stayed heavy, stayed vicious.

I jumped on him immediately with a savage ground and pound against the cage. I was sharp, relentless and unforgiving. I punched him up properly and made it clear that he was not going to be escaping this. He tried to cover up but just couldn't fight back. The ref watched closely, "Defend yourself!" he said, but he couldn't. The punches had broken him mentally and physically, and he slumped, defeated. By the time the round ended, he knew it was all over. He couldn't continue, a TKO and the fight stopped.

I didn't care how it came, there are no fairytales in war. I had done what I needed to do and could proudly say I was champion. The emotion hit me instantly, I spun around and charged to the cage wall, jumping up and perching on top like a king. The crowd went INSANE. Phones were out everywhere, people cheering, the block roaring - the whole arena was shaking.

I roared from the top, "THIS IS MY CAGE!"

The energy was wild. Madness everywhere. It was real. I let it soak in. I stayed up there for a second, my chest heaving, eyes scanning the whole arena. The king was home. I dropped back down, and they wrapped the belt around my waist. The weight of it hit different, it was solid. I had earnt this.

I looked down at it, "Yeah… this is mine now" I thought to myself. This wasn't hype anymore, or about proving doubters wrong, now this was about legacy. As I walked backstage I had a chance to re-flect properly. The old me, all those setbacks, the triangle scare, pocket war, shoulder pop, punches, it all came rushing back, yet the thing that stood out was the roar from the crowd, and now I was crowned.

I wasn't just Marcus, I wasn't just Maddog from the block, I was Mad-dog the Champion. Deep down I knew this wasn't the end but only the beginning.

CHAPTER FOURTEEN

DOUBLE OR NOTHING

Winning the belt should have silenced everyone, but in this game, it's never that simple. Even after being crowned, whispers still floated around, "Yeah, but his opponent's shoulder popped", "Would he have really won without that?", "Was it actually a clean victory?"

I didn't care much, but I heard it everywhere. The respect felt half-hearted and while half of the people rated it, the other half doubted it. That's how fighting goes. You don't earn respect through belts, you earn it through violence and consistency. I knew I couldn't sit back and relax. This was no time for rest or for showing off the belt like a trophy. I couldn't afford to go missing now, which is why I stayed locked in.

So when the next opportunity came fast, another fight, another show, another belt on the line, I accepted straight away. This wasn't just another match-up, it was my shot to become double champion and to shut everyone up properly by putting real weight behind my name.

Of course I said yes. That was never a question. But the opponent? He made things personal before we even stepped into the cage. From the moment the fight was announced, he ran his mouth heavy, "Maddog? Nah. He only won because of luck. Shoulder injury saved him." "He ain't legit. He can't beat a real fighter like me." "I'm going to smash him up and show who the real champ is."

The talking didn't stop.

Podcasts. Interviews. Social media. Even backstage at the weigh-ins - everywhere I turned, I heard the same energy. "Expose Maddog, take his spot." But I stayed calm. Stayed cold. I didn't care about replying, I didn't need to prove anything through words. The cage would do the talking for me.

When fight night arrived, the energy in the arena was heavy. This wasn't like my past fights, there was tension everywhere. Everyone in there knew what was on the line. If I won, I would be a double champion with an undoubted legacy. If I lost though, then people would call me a fake, just another temporary hype job.

Despite the pressure, I wasn't nervous. I remained serious. The walk-out felt different. There was no hype or ego, just pure purpose. As I stood across from him, I saw it in his face, he really believed he was going to break me. He really thought he was about to take everything I worked for.

The ref brought us in, "Ready?" I nodded. "Ready?" He nodded. The bell rang.

Twenty seconds later, it was over. He rushed forward instantly. It was wild and reckless, and he thought he could bully me early and put pressure on. Bad move. I stayed sharp, letting him come forward and timed it perfectly. I clinched, dragging him to the ground and locking him in a tight guillotine choke.

It was deep. Real deep.

I felt him panic almost instantly. The same mouth that had been speaking loudly all week was now struggling for air. There was no space. No escape. He tapped fast, less than twenty seconds and I had secured a submission win. Just like that, I was victorious again and crowned double champion.

I didn't celebrate wildly or scream in his face. I just stood there, cold, calm, and collected with two belts over my shoulders. All that talk? All that hype? All that disrespect? Silenced. Gone. Forgotten.

Now it was simple, I was Maddog the Double Champion. This time there was no question of luck or being gifting it. I had earned it. Four wins in a row, a 6-3 record. People used to say I couldn't do this, that I was just a brawler or wasn't technical enough. That I was no good on the ground, but they were wrong. I have proved people wrong every single time. I submitted opponents, I finished fights, and I made champions quit.

Now, standing with two belts on my shoulders, the question wasn't "Can Maddog do this?" but instead, "What's next?" Because right now, sitting in front of me was one more amateur title opportunity and if I took it I would become a triple champion, an undisputed fighter. Or was it already time to say goodbye to amateur ranks and step up to the big world by going pro and showing the whole planet who Maddog was?

The decision weighed heavy in my mind. One more belt, or the biggest step of my career? That answer wasn't clear yet. But what was clear was that whoever stood across from me next had better be ready because this wasn't the end of my story, I was only just getting warmed up.

TO BE CONTINUED.

ABOUT THE AUTHOR

Marcus "Maddog" Morgan is more than just a name — he's a survivor, a fighter, and a voice from the shadows. Born and raised in the heart of Smethwick, Marcus carved his reputation through the chaos of street life, gang wars, and years behind prison walls. What began in violence evolved into victory as he rebuilt himself in the cage, turning pain into purpose through MMA. Now a double amateur champion and rising star, Maddog is also a storyteller, using music and memoir to lay bare the unfiltered truth of a life rebuilt. His journey from block soldier to cage king isn't just about fighting — it's about legacy. Maddog: Built for War is his first book, and it's only the beginning.

Instagram maddog_mma1

Tiktok maddogmma1

YouTube MD Maddog.

Maddogmma

GLOSSARY OF TERMS

Block – The local area or estate. Represents more than geography — it's where loyalty, hustle, and danger all live.

Mandem – Slang for a close crew or group of trusted friends, usually from the streets.

Shotting – Selling drugs. Used to describe street-level hustle.

Strap – A firearm.

Burner – An untraceable mobile phone, typically used for street activity or in jail to avoid detection.

Ops – Short for "opposition" or enemies, usually rival crews or gangs.

On your toes / Ghosted – To be alert and moving carefully to avoid police or detection.

Screws – Prison officers or guards.

Segregation / The Block – Isolation unit in prison. Used to punish or control inmates.

Patterned – To handle a situation effectively or set something up well. "I patterned them quickly" = I dealt with them fast.

Clout – Street respect or notoriety, especially when earned through action.

Maddog – Marcus's alter ego and street/fight name. More than a nickname, it represents fearlessness, loyalty, and raw survival instinct.

PART 2 TEASER IN BUILT FOR WAR

🔥 COMING NEXT

BORN FOR WAR

Before the Cage, There Was Only Violence

You've seen the fighter I became.
Now see the chaos that created him.

From broken homes to broken rules —
Born for War is the savage prequel to this story.

Printed in Dunstable, United Kingdom

64044778R00030